Far Above Rubies

VIRTUE
JOURNAL

BY KIMBERLY A. MUCKER-JOHNSON, MECHELLE ROBERSON, CASSANDRA TEMBO, PEGGY BENNETT, DEBORAH EVANS, AND TERA LYNN HOUSTON

Qui Docet Discit Publishing, LLC
Louisville, KY 40272
quidocetdiscitpublishing@gmail.com

ISBN 13: 978-1-953376-06-0

Dedication

Giving honor to our Lord and Savior Jesus Christ. The development and implementation of Women In Search of Excellence (W.I.S.E) Talk has helped us to grow and to learn as a sisterhood and as individuals. We found people that we can be transparent and feel safe with. We wrote and designed this journal for you. We are not interested in any vainglory for ourselves, but we have humbly submitted ourselves to answer the calling to be transparent in order to connect with other Sisters! It is our deepest hope and prayer that this journal will find you wherever you are and bring healing in the name of Jesus Christ. We hope that in our brokenness, you can be healed. We have already prayed for you, and will continue to pray with you throughout this journey. We love you, Sis!

Table of Contents

Introduction

As long as we have breath in this body, we are on a journey. On this journey, some days feel like a walk in the park. Other days feel like a roller coaster. Still other days, we dance in the rain. Yet, there are days when we feel as if we are walking alone in a horrible storm. All of these days are a "course" ordained by God before we were even formed in our mother's womb. "I knew you before I formed you in your mother's womb. Before you were born I set you apart and appointed you as my prophet to the nations" (Jeremiah 1:5 NLT). It is God who decided the purpose, your gifts, and your days. He decided when you would be born, during what time period, to what parents, and even the color of your skin.

The words "journal" and "journey" are derived from the same root, the French word, "jour," which means "day." **A journal takes place daily. It is a daily trip or work. It is a daily** self-examination or reflection. The journey is the hyphen on your obituary. It's the daily die (1 Corinthians 15:31; Romans 8:36). It is the grace to deny self, to take up your cross daily, and to follow Him (Luke 9:23). Everyday that you wake up with breath in your body, you have a new day, new mercies to do the will of the Lord. You have a new start. It is our advice "to work the hyphen" through self-examinations. For if we would judge ourselves, we should not be judged (1 Corinthians 11:31). At this point, maybe you're wondering, *what do I judge or how do I judge myself*. You are to judge the fruit in your life using the standard - *The Word of the Lord*. You are to become a fruit inspector of your fruit or lack thereof.

"Virtue" is the feminine version of the adjective "valor". Virtue is moral strength, high character, goodness, and excellence. Virtues are characteristics that promote collective and individual greatness. Virtue is described as strength from straining, stretching, and extending. We see this in the Proverbs 31 woman. She embodies all of these important traits as she lives out her everyday life. Every woman I know has desired to be a virtuous woman. Yes, we acknowledge that the character traits of a virtuous woman are desirable, but we must also accept that we cannot be virtuous in our own strength as many of us have already tried to be a *Super Woman*. Therefore, the most important aspect of virtue is voluntary submission to the one true God, and as submitted vessels, we are to think on "...whatever things are true, whatever things are noble, whatever things are just, whatever things are pure, whatever things are lovely, whatever things are of good report, if there is any virtue and if there is anything praiseworthy—meditate on these things" (Philippians 4:8).

Fruit..it was fruit that put the whole human race in this deathtrap called sin. It was the fruit of Jesus that paid the price fully and once and for all which redeemed us. It is the fruit of the Lord that gives us free will to choose Him. We read the parable of the fig tree in Luke 13:6-9:

> "And he told this parable: "A man had a fig tree planted in his vineyard, and he came seeking fruit on it and found none. And he said to the vinedresser, 'Look, for three years now I have come seeking fruit on this fig tree, and I find none. Cut it down. Why should it use up the ground?' And he answered him, 'Sir, let it alone this year also, until I dig around it and put on manure. Then if it should bear fruit next year, well and good; but if not, you can cut it down".

We are the fig tree. It's only by God's grace and mercy that we have not been cut down. We need to bear fruit. Jesus has already completed his part by digging around us and fertilizing us with manure. We must repent, quench the drought, and bear fruit as we have been ordained to do.

In Galatians 5:22-23 (NLT), we read about the "fruits of virtue" or the fruit of the Spirit: "But the Holy Spirit produces this kind of fruit in our lives: love, joy, peace, patience, kindness, goodness, faithfulness, gentleness, and self-control." There is no law against these things!" It is good news that we don't have to produce fruit on our own. The Holy Ghost produces them. We do have to turn over our free will. We do have to give an **UNCONDITIONAL YES**.

Who can find a virtuous woman? For her price is far above rubies. The Bible teaches us to give "...all diligence, add to your faith virtue, to virtue knowledge, to knowledge self-control, to self-control perseverance, to perseverance godliness, to godliness brotherly kindness, and to brotherly kindness love" (1 Peter 1:5-7). Virtue helps add to our faith, to our knowledge, to our self-control, to our perseverance, to our godliness, to our brotherly kindness and to our brotherly love. You are not your own source of virtue. God is our only source. You don't have that kind of power within you. It is only the divine power of God that can produce the fruit of virtue, and then virtue multiplied gives us fruit, more fruit, and much fruit.

But the Holy Spirit produces this kind of fruit in our lives: love, joy, peace, patience, kindness, goodness, faithfulness, gentleness, and self-control. There is no law against these things!

Galatians 5:22-23 (NLT)

LOVE
LOVE
LOVE

FOR GOD SO LOVED THE WORLD...
JOHN 3:16

LOVE
LOVE
LOVE

FOR GOD SO LOVED THE WORLD...
JOHN 3:16

Love
By Peggy Bennett

Love is the first and the greatest commandment. Love must be very important to God as it's mentioned in the King James version 508 times in the Old Testament and 697 in the New Testament. John 4:7-9 (NIV) says, "Beloved, let us love one another, for love is of God; and everyone who loves is born of God and knows God. He who does not love does not know God, for God is love. In this the love of God was manifested toward us, that God has sent His only begotten Son into the world, that we might live through Him. Luke 10:27 (NIV) tells us that we should, "...love the Lord your God with all your heart, with all your soul, with all your strength, and with all your mind, and your neighbor as yourself. " We learn in 1 Corinthians 13:3-8 (MSG), "If I give everything I own to the poor and even go to the stake to be burned as a martyr, but I don't love, I've gotten nowhere. So, no matter what I say, what I believe, and what I do, I'm bankrupt without love. Love never gives up. Love cares more for others than for self. Love doesn't want what it doesn't have. Love doesn't strut, Doesn't have a swelled head, Doesn't force itself on others, Isn't always "me first," Doesn't fly off the handle, Doesn't keep score of the sins of others, Doesn't revel when others grovel, Takes pleasure in the flowering of truth, Puts up with anything, Trusts God always, Always looks for the best, Never looks back, But keeps going to the end. Love never dies."

Do you love Jesus?

To understand what it means to love Jesus, we must first define what is meant by the word *love*. Since we are discussing Jesus, we will limit our definitions to the two primary Greek words used for **"love"** in the New Testament. The first is **philia**. This refers to a brotherly love or to a close association with another person. To demonstrate this type of love would not require any substantial sacrifice on the part of the lover. This love is shown through a cordial attitude and an allotment of time. Anyone from a mild acquaintance to a close colleague can be loved with **philia**. This type of love will easily fade, especially if the loved one moves away or is not often encountered. Thus, this is not the type of love that would be adequate for the kind of love Jesus wants from His followers. The other Greek word for "love" is **agape** which is the love I will focus on here. This type of love is considered unconditional love. This is the love that Paul describes in 1 Corinthians 13, and is most appropriate for understanding what it means to love Jesus. Paul explains this type of love by what it does and what it doesn't do. **Agape** love is patient, kind, rejoicing with truth, bearing all things, believing all things, hoping in all things, and enduring through all things. In contrast, *agape* does not envy, boast, or rejoice in wrongdoing; it is not arrogant, rude, selfish, irritable, or resentful. Most importantly, *agape* love does not end. It will not fade away like **philia** *love*. **Agape** love is not based on circumstances and will never end. To love the Lord is to follow Him wherever He leads, to obey Him in whatever He asks, and to trust Him in whatever the trial may be. To love Jesus is to reflect the love that God has for us. **Agape** love is not based on emotion but on the will. Each characteristic of **agape** love is a deliberate choice to act in a certain manner. Thus, when Jesus said, "If you love me, you will keep my commandments" (John 14:15), He was teaching that loving Him would be a demonstrable action not an emotional feeling. If Jesus is to be loved as He commanded, then a conscious choice must be made to act according to the pattern described in 1 Corinthians 13. Jesus was clear that loving Him is a service and that disobedience is a lack of love. Therefore, to love Jesus is to willfully act in such a way that our devotion to Him is proven through our actions toward Him and our obedience of Him.

How do you fall in love with Jesus?

The same way you fall in love with a human being. When that person shows interest in you, and you show interest back. Someone initiates a conversation and begins investing their time. Talking to God becomes a priority because there's something there that you don't understand but you know you just want more. Sometimes He may write you a love letter, and you read that letter over and over. You may even write Him a love letter back. You make God a priority in your life, and begin carving time out of your daily routine because you want more of Him. You want His attention, you want His love, you want to know who He is and how He works. You sacrifice something *here* to show you care more for Him than *that,* and you give up something *there* because you want to know what will happen if you spend just one more hour with Him now. You share your secrets with God. You tell Him the best parts and the worst parts. The more you allow God to love you, the more you will receive His **agape** love and extend that same love to others.

About 30 years ago I was challenged in many ways to either allow pain and hurt to destroy my very being or to show agape love towards those who had inflicted the pain. I felt that my heart had been broken up into a million pieces time after time. It's impossible to forgive and to show agape love to those who have caused pain in your life without the help of the Lord. I'm reminded of the story of Joseph in how he could have chosen to get even with his brother for all the hurtful things they did to him, but instead he chose to forgive them, "You intended to harm me, but God intended it for good to accomplish what is now being done, the saving of many lives" (Genesis 50: 20). Loving those who have hurt us is a direct result of the love of God. Loving in an *agape* way is manifested in us by changing us to be more like God, and insofar as we are changed. We allow God's love to work in us and through the divine *agape* we can forgive and be united with those who have hurt us. Remember loving our enemies is only possible when we are filled with God's love, content to be in His presence, and not worried or fearful about the outcome of our actions. In order to love in a *agape* way those who may have caused harm to you, one must forgive that person first. Of course, this is not easy for us,but Our Lord will give you the grace to do His will if we ask it of Him. Trust Him today by saying a prayer for that person who has hurt you. Pray for grace to forgive and to show agape love to that person in spite of their actions. Watch the power of prayer make what may have seemed impossible possible even for our fallen human hearts. Pray for a closer relationship with Jesus and to receive His agape love.

Love Prayer for My Sister

Dear Lord, I have been hurt very deeply by individuals who I thought truly loved me. Restore my brokenness I pray, and send Your comfort and strength into my soul as I try to pick up the pieces of my brokenness and begin to face the future once again. Lord, I know that I cannot do this in my own strength, but only as You carry me in Your loving arms and pour Your healing and comfort into my broken soul. In You is the fullness of joy and from You alone comes the only true agape love that can fully satisfy the heart that is hungry for love. I pray that I may allow the healing process of Your agape love to begin to mend my brokenness. Help me to pray, "Thy will be done," in every area of my life and to teach me how to love You as I ought. Give me the capacity to love others in an agape way as You have loved me. In Jesus' name I pray. Amen.

LOVE
LOVE LOVE
LOVE

FOR GOD SO LOVED THE WORLD...
JOHN 3:16

MIRROR MOMENT

A
AFFECT
(EMOTIONS)

B
BEHAVIOR
(ACTIONS)

C
COGNITION
(THOUGHTS)

~Reflections ~

SOAP BIBLE STUDY METHOD

S - Scripture

Read the scripture without trying to determine meaning. Just read what is there.

O - Observance

Notice what stands out for you or what captures your attention. Sometimes, using the 5 W's helps with this – who, what, when, where, why, and how?

A - Application

Ask yourself, "so what?" How does this apply to me and my life and how can I utilize it in my life?" Be honest with yourself.

P - Prayer

Pray without ceasing. Pray before. Pray during. Pray afterwards. Be prayerful throughout this process.

SOAP BIBLE STUDY METHOD

S - Scripture

O - Observance

A - Application

P - Prayer

SCRIPTURES ON THIS FRUIT

SEEDS TO PRODUCE MUCH FRUIT

Compass Points

What action(s) were taken? What action(s) do you need to take?

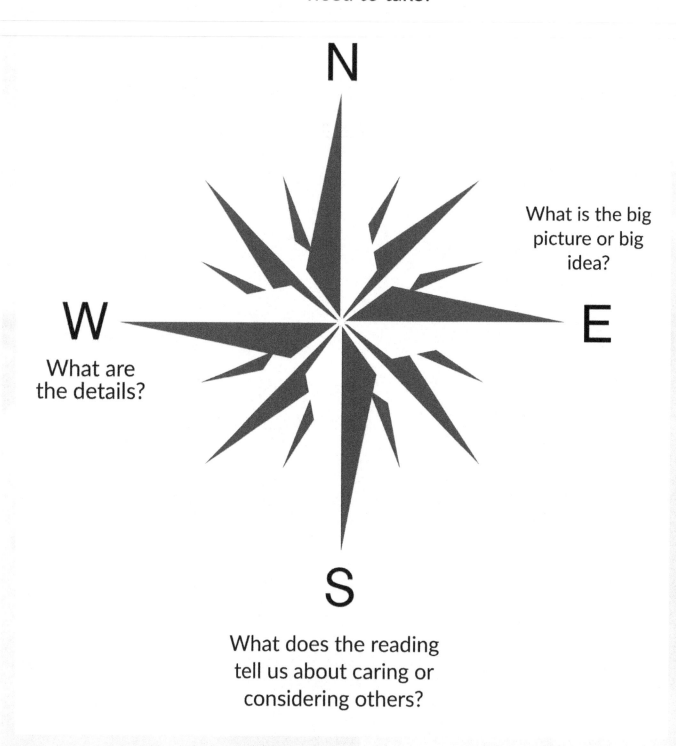

N

E

What is the big picture or big idea?

W

What are the details?

S

What does the reading tell us about caring or considering others?

Note to self

K
What do you know?

W
What do you want to know?

L
What did you learn?

Made in the image of God

Month:

Month:

Joy

THE JOY OF THE LORD IS MY STRENGTH
- NEHEMIAH 8:10

Joy

THE JOY OF THE LORD IS MY STRENGTH
- NEHEMIAH 8:10

Joy
By Tera Lynn Houston

The book of Nehemiah is one of my favorite books of the Bible. While serving as cupbearer to the King in Persia, Nehemiah received word that things weren't going so well back home in Judah. The walls of Jerusalem were torn down and the remnant of people left living in Judah was in distress. The state of the walls left the city in a vulnerable position without social or economic stability and open to attack. Nehemiah was obviously burdened by the circumstances back home so much that the King noticed and inquired of him the reason for his despair. After discussing the state of affairs, King Artaxerxes granted Nehemiah permission to return to his hometown to fortify and to rebuild the walls. Although Nehemiah was burdened, he knew the promises of God to restore the land. God again proved His faithfulness by moving upon the heart of a pagan King to accomplish His sovereign plans and purposes for His people. During the seventh month on the first day, Ezra, the scribe, brought forth the book of the law of Moses before the congregation of both men and women at their request. Ezra read the Word of God for six hours to the people from daybreak till noon. The Israelites recognized the value of the Word of God and stood up in reverence as the Word went forth. Leaders led small groups explaining the Word to the people as they wept realizing their previous refusal to hear had caused several years of delay. In verse ten of chapter 8, Nehemiah encourages the people not to mourn nor weep: "For the joy of the Lord is your strength." His instructions could be paraphrased as "Do not grieve, focus on the Lord; He'll give you joy and strength."

Joy is often used as the acronym for Jesus, Yourself, Others. I do not necessarily disagree with that description, and I particularly agree with placing Jesus first and foremost in our circumstances and daily life. In my opinion, keeping Jesus as our focus gives us proper perspective which leads to proper direction, actions, and reactions. Oftentimes, joy is mistaken for happiness and used interchangeably despite very significant differences. Happiness is external, temporal, and by chance. Happiness comes and goes based upon circumstances and is dependent upon and reactive to things out of our control. You can be happy one moment, and unhappy the next because happiness is a fleeting emotion. On the contrary, the fruit of the spirit joy is not circumstantial but intentional. Joy is a deliberate choice and determination to praise God in all circumstances and situations. Knowing that God is in full control of our lives allows us to be confident that everything will be alright (Romans 8:28). Even if our circumstances don't change, God's purpose and plan for our lives will prevail. Nothing is wasted in our lives…the good, the bad, and the ugly can all be used for our good and His glory. Because our eyes and heart are focused on Christ, we can have joy no matter what situation we find ourselves in. Joy is not temporal but it remains. I'm reminded of the scripture John 15:11 (NKJV), "These things I have spoken to you, that My joy may remain in you, and that your joy may be full."

When researching English language descriptions of joy, I found things such as feelings of great pleasure and happiness. Merriam Webster dictionary defines it as an emotion evoked by well-being, success, good fortune, or by a prospect of possessing what one desires. I found how joy is described in the English language and the western worldview's as limited and external when I compared it to how joy is described in the Bible. Psalm 105:43 discusses the Israelites' joy in the wilderness experience. In Philippians 3:1, while in prison Paul talks about having joy in the Lord. David in Psalm

5:11 encourages the reader to be joyful in God. Paul again encourages in 2 Corinthians 6:10 to be joyful in sorrow and always rejoicing, which implies that we have nothing yet we own everything. This is only possible through joy.

While reflecting over my life, there are many situations in which I had to choose joy despite external circumstances. Early in our marriage, like many young couples, my husband and I struggled financially. Very young and newly married while learning to navigate the waters of being part of a blended family was very challenging. Simultaneously, while learning to "blend" our blended family, unbeknownst to myself, I was grappling with my own feelings as an adult regarding the absence and rejection of my biological father. A few years later, my husband and I had our son after enduring a high-risk pregnancy. Those nine months were filled with doctor visits, specialists, ultrasounds, steroid shots, etc. These were some of the most stressful, uncertain, and frightening times of my life. To top it all off, I was in horrific pain a great deal of the time during my pregnancy and was placed on bed rest several weeks - initially at home,then ultimately in the hospital. Time spent in the hospital was very tiring and lonely. One day after returning home from a specialist visit, I became very overwhelmed from their report. I remember crying out to God while lying on the couch alone in my apartment. I decided to pray about my situation regarding my pregnancy and unborn baby and leave it in God's hands knowing that if he so chose to, he could take care of me and my baby despite what the doctor reported. After praying and crying out, I felt such peace like never before. My circumstances had not changed. I was still high risk according to doctors, BUT my perspective and focus had changed. I no longer focused on my problems but on WHO God was - His faithfulness, His attributes, and His ability to supersede and intervene in my situation which He did. I once read about a race car driving instructor teaching someone to drive. The instructor advised the student on the best way to come out of a spin if he loses control of the car. "Focus on where you want to end up not on the spin itself because what you focus on you'll hit." That resonated with me and still does to this day. I have learned that having joy doesn't mean to suppress pain or sorrow, nor does it mean to be complacent or lazy while being content in all circumstances. We should still seek God's purposes for our lives and be in prayer for our next moves and steps following His lead and guidance. However, don't focus on your problems or circumstances; focus on God and be obedient to His call and direction. By doing so you can rest assured you will have fullness of joy.

Joy Prayer for My Sister

Dear Heavenly Father, I lift up my sister reading this before you right now. May she not be overcome by negative circumstances while she pursues and seeks Your will and purpose for her life. Let her not be discouraged by what is seen but rather encouraged by what cannot be seen; Lord, show her that her faith in you isn't dependent upon good conditions. My sister, trust in who you know God is - His holy nature, faithful character, and attributes. "I have told you these things so that My joy may be in you, and that your joy may be full." – John 15:11

MIRROR MOMENT

A
AFFECT
(EMOTIONS)

B
BEHAVIOR
(ACTIONS)

C
COGNITION
(THOUGHTS)

~Reflections ~

SOAP BIBLE STUDY METHOD

S - Scripture

Read the scripture without trying to determine meaning. Just read what is there.

O - Observance

Notice what stands out for you or what captures your attention. Sometimes, using the 5 W's helps with this – who, what, when, where, why, and how?

A - Application

Ask yourself, "so what?" How does this apply to me and my life and how can I utilize it in my life?" Be honest with yourself.

P - Prayer

Pray without ceasing. Pray before. Pray during. Pray afterwards. Be prayerful throughout this process.

SOAP BIBLE STUDY METHOD

S - Scripture

O - Observance

A - Application

P - Prayer

SCRIPTURES ON THIS FRUIT

SEEDS TO PRODUCE MUCH FRUIT

Compass Points

What action(s) were taken? What action(s) do you
need to take?

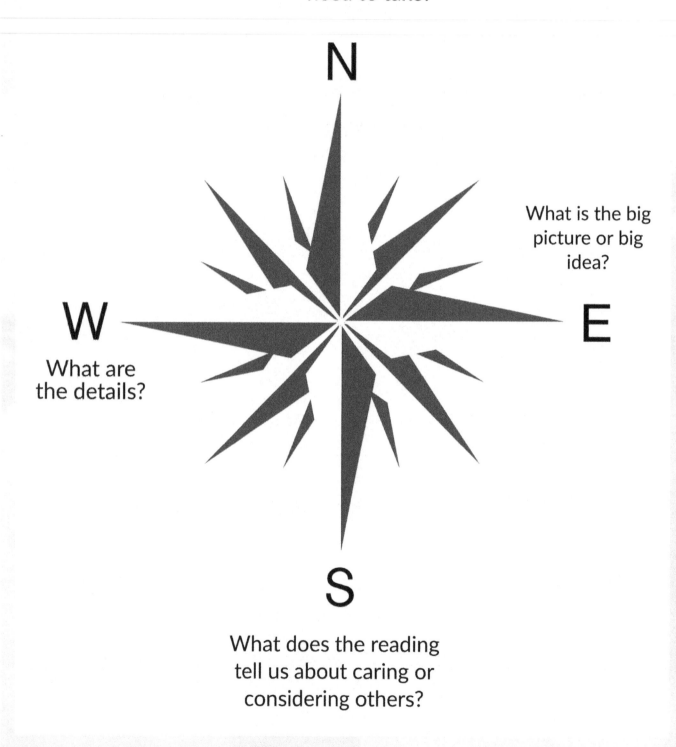

N

What is the big
picture or big
idea?

E

W

What are
the details?

S

What does the reading
tell us about caring or
considering others?

Note to self

K
What do you know?

W
What do you want to know?

L
What did you learn?

Made in the image of God

Month:

Month:

PEACE

John 14:27

PEACE I LEAVE WITH YOU; MY PEACE I GIVE YOU. I DO NOT GIVE TO YOU AS THE WORLD GIVES. DO NOT LET YOUR HEARTS BE TROUBLED AND DO NOT BE AFRAID.

PEACE

John 14:27

PEACE I LEAVE WITH YOU; MY PEACE I GIVE YOU. I DO NOT
GIVE TO YOU AS THE WORLD GIVES. DO NOT LET YOUR HEARTS BE TROUBLED AND DO NOT BE AFRAID.

Peace

By Deborah Evans

John 14:27 "Peace I leave with you, my peace I give unto you: not as the world giveth, give I unto you. Let not your heart be troubled, neither let it be afraid".

During my life of chaos, yelling, screaming, cussing and fussing, I desired peace. I wasn't sure exactly what that meant, but I just knew that if I would keep myself busy and occupied, then I could perhaps escape in my mind to a place of quietness. I remember creating homework for myself, reading and writing papers on what I read, or even working math problems just to keep busy. This was not for school, and it did not just happen during school days/season, but it took place during the summer. I remember one summer, I was determined to teach myself to type using the manual typewriter and a workbook. And that's what I did.

On my spiritual journey, I have learned that God is intentional and strategic. He tells us what to do, how to prepare because He knew from the beginning what we were going to face in our lifetime. In the scripture above, why did Jesus mention leaving peace as He prepared to ascend back to Heaven? Why did He tell us to not let our hearts be troubled or fearful? If He mentioned peace, then it's a very important fruit to partake of, to digest, and to give attention to.

I thought I knew what peace meant, or I knew what it meant to me. Although each fruit of the spirit is detrimental to our spiritual walk while on earth, peace seemed to be the one that stood out for me, especially in the recent years. Online dictionaries define "shalom" as a Hebrew word meaning peace, harmony, wholeness, completeness, prosperity, welfare and tranquility. One online dictionary states that peace is a stress-free state of security and calmness that comes when there's no fighting or war, and everything coexisting in perfect harmony and freedom. One of the most quoted scriptures on peace is Philippians 4:7 , "And the peace of God, which passeth (surpasses, exceeds, be greater than) all understanding..." gives us an idea about the type of peace which comes from God.

The peace that the world gives is temporary and dependent on time such as how much time you can get away, or when you're on your job, escaping to your car for 30 minutes. But the peace that God gives is everlasting! It's supernatural (above what's normal)! It's the type of peace that can sustain you when you are in the middle of the chaos. The kind of peace that not even you can understand at times. Peace is knowing that God will never leave you nor forsake you .

God said to us in scripture that He came to give us life more abundantly. For so long, I interpreted abundance as stuff or things. I have learned that allowing us to have our right mind is abundance. So many of us have gone through heartaches, disappointments, betrayals, uncertainties, loss, hurt, and pain. These hard times should have made us lose our minds. And even if we did lose our minds, it is the peace of the Lord that restores us. Our Lord is a mind regulator!

The word peace is mentioned in both the Old and New Testament about 420 times, so that means that it's a necessary virtue that we need in order to remain whole on this Spiritual journey. With all that God has commanded that we possess, it's not forced, it is a conscious decision and choice that each of us have to say yes - an unconditional yes! For it's for our good, and the glorification of our God. This unconditional yes is necessary to walk in peace, to desire peace, to be the author of peace and to declare peace in your life. It's a matter of life and death!

Sometimes walking in peace may require being quiet. Not saying a word even when you know you are right. In Exodus 14:14, Moses tells the children of Israel, "The Lord will fight for you; you need only to be still." I was in a situation where I was betrayed by someone that I thought loved me and would fight for me. I had to sit there in the midst of what I interpreted as an attack of my person, my reputation, my family and my child, and not challenge my foe (a person who feels enmity, hatred, or malice toward another person) with some truths. I sat there feeling abandoned and thinking...***Lord, if you don't help me now, then I'll have a lot of repenting to do*** (transparency)! I was amazed at how I did not feel the need to hurt someone who I was connected to at one time in life - genuine on my end. When it was over, I took a long drive, just praying and asking God for direction. I needed to know what to do. My thought was that I must run since I did not fight. But God reminded me that the battle was not mine and that He would keep my mind in perfect peace (Isaiah 26:3) in the midst of pain and confusion. I finally went home still having to go to work but could not sleep a wink. All I could do was pray and present my issues at the throne of our God. As the sun rose, darkness now turning into light (day), I showered, dressed and went to work. This is what peace did for me, **God's peace**, I worked the entire eight hours without being sleepy or tired, and more importantly, my heart was not bitter. The following night, I slept in peace because I knew that I was safe with and in God (Psalms 4:8).

What I learned about myself and God is by believing in His

word and seeking peace in every aspect of my life that He will give you just what you need, even when you do not know what you need. God never intended for us to be alone or to go through disappointments, betrayal, hurt, pain, trauma, defeat, setbacks, or to just do life without Him. He knew what we needed, and His peace allows us to fellowship with one another, to pray for one another, and to incorporate peace in our relationships with each other. Through experiences, we become capable of demonstrating and digesting the fruit of the Spirit in its entirety. It is so necessary.

In order to possess this kind of peace, it requires an unconditional yes as I mentioned above. How do you give this unconditional yes? Choose God daily, read His word, pray and be specific in your prayer, fast and God will reveal you to you, so you will know what you are lacking, and then you act on it. I sought peace and found it. I also realize that we don't have to ask for peace, it's there. Just walk in it, live a righteous life and peace comes, then you will rest in a peaceful place (Isaiah 32:16-17).

While writing this, my mother was in a nursing facility during this Covid-19 pandemic. I could not see her in person. My mother suffered a stroke in September 2019, which left her paralyzed on the left side of her body. Prior to the stroke, she had stopped eating, and she would only eat when I sat down and pretty much fed her a little at a time. What compounded the situation is in 2011-2012, she was diagnosed with dementia, which could have been responsible for the eating situation. With that said, after the stroke, my mother was sent to rehab to help her to possibly walk again, to get some usage out of her left limbs again, etc. However, with dementia, responding to therapy made it impossible for her to grasp therapy and work on the exercises that would help her regain some liberty. In addition, they recommended a feeding tube to help her regain her strength, and to possibly be able to respond to therapy. The therapy did not change her condition nor did the feeding tube, so long term care was recommended for her. During this process, we were at the hospital/nursing facility every day. In fact, I would spend my entire Saturday at the nursing home, and also after church on Sundays. I would have been there during the week, but I had to work, be a wife, and attend my son's sporting events. When I would go to the nursing home, I would brush my mother's teeth, clean her nails, stroll her in her wheelchair around the facility, bathe her, change her, lotion her entire body, try to feed her (the feeding tube was supposed to have been temporary), coerce her into sipping her favorite drink, sweet tea, through a straw, talk to her, clean her room, wash her clothes and make sure she was taken care of when we weren't there. Then one day in March 2020, I went to the nursing facility and was met with signs on the door that stated I could not visit my Mom. My heart dropped and immediately I was feeling all kinds of anxieties. So I had to go to what I knew worked - pray, pray and PRAY! I knew that her needs were not going to be met because I couldn't take care of her. I prayed, prayed and prayed some more. God gave me peace to keep my mind. He gave me peace, which kept me from worrying about her care. Peace gave me hope. I had peace to remind me that angels were encamped around my mother every day and night. It was peace that I prayed would consume my Mother's thoughts. Peace that the nurses and nurse assistants would not forget about her. I learned to trust God even more because peace of mind freed me to put total trust in God. The fact that He loves us enough to make sure that "all is well". This peace is invaluable! It cannot be duplicated or replaced. It's a part of living life in abundance. And it's not just for me but you too can have this peace. My mother passed away on November 16, 2020. May God continue to give me peace even though I cannot see her, touch her, and take care of her anymore, but I know she is at peace and I have the peace of God.

Peace Prayer for My Sister

Father God, I come to you with a grateful heart for the person who has read my personal testimony about your peace and how this fruit will enhance their life and the lives around them. God, I pray that the person reading this passage will have a heart to receive what you intended for them before they were formed in their mother's womb. Lord God, I pray that you give us the desire to seek peace, to live in peace, to walk in peace and to be peacemakers for your Glory as it will be for our good! Lord, give us the willingness to let go of the temporary and superficial peace that the world gives and seek the peace that surpasses all understanding which only comes from you. Lord, keep their minds in perfect peace. Let us crave your peace daily and in every situation. God, please give us the desire to want the same peace for our foes and enemies. Lord, give us a spirit of an unconditional yes that we may be healed, delivered and set free. Lord, give us a desire to seek your wisdom through your word, seek you in prayer, and seek you in our actions. Lord, let us find refuge in you - the peaceful place. Lord I bind up, in Jesus Name, those spirits that would block our peace and loose the presence and the Spirit of God, spirit of repentance and the spirit of peace in our lives for you said what's bound in heaven shall be bound on earth and what's loosed in heaven shall be loosed on earth, and I claim it done in Jesus' Name! Amen.

PEACE

John 14:27

PEACE I LEAVE WITH YOU; MY PEACE I GIVE YOU. I DO NOT
GIVE TO YOU AS THE WORLD GIVES. DO NOT LET YOUR HEARTS BE TROUBLED AND DO NOT BE AFRAID.

MIRROR MOMENT

A
AFFECT
(EMOTIONS)

B
BEHAVIOR
(ACTIONS)

C
COGNITION
(THOUGHTS)

~Reflections ~

SOAP BIBLE STUDY METHOD

S – Scripture

Read the scripture without trying to determine meaning. Just read what is there.

O – Observance

Notice what stands out for you or what captures your attention. Sometimes, using the 5 W's helps with this – who, what, when, where, why, and how?

A – Application

Ask yourself, "so what?" How does this apply to me and my life and how can I utilize it in my life?" Be honest with yourself.

P – Prayer

Pray without ceasing. Pray before. Pray during. Pray afterwards. Be prayerful throughout this process.

S - Scripture   O - Observance

A - Application   P - Prayer

SCRIPTURES ON THIS FRUIT

SEEDS TO PRODUCE MUCH FRUIT

Compass Points

What action(s) were taken? What action(s) do you need to take?

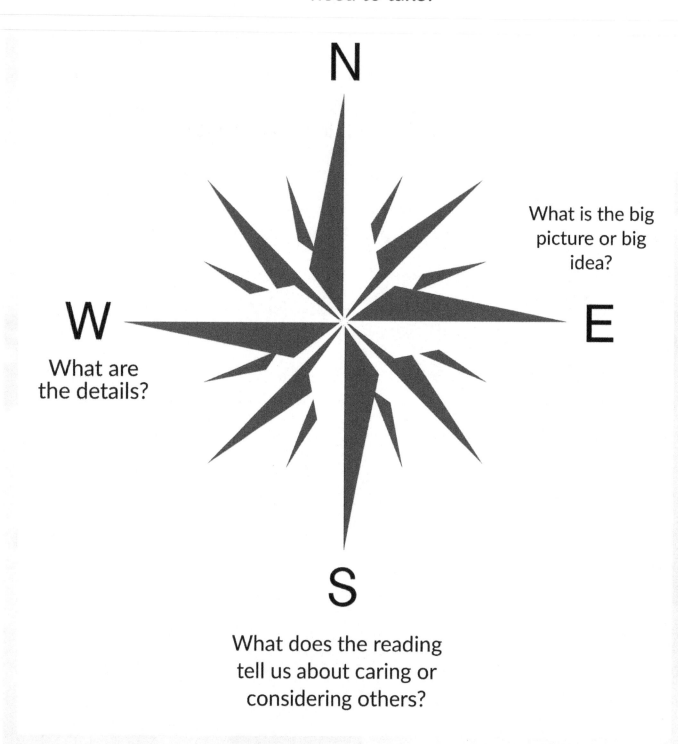

N

What is the big picture or big idea?

E

W

What are the details?

S

What does the reading tell us about caring or considering others?

Note to self

K
What do you know?

W
What do you want to know?

L
What did you learn?

Made in the image of God

Month:

Month:

PATIENCE

But if we hope for what we do not see, we wait for it with patience.

#Romans825

PATIENCE.

But if we hope for
what we do not
see, we wait for
it with patience.

#Romans825

Patience

By Cassandra Tembo

I often think about Albertina Walker and James Cleveland's song, "Please Be Patient with Me". If you are not familiar with this song, then look it up and even listen to it online. The words of this song convey a plea that in the event the person is seen or heard in a light that does not reflect God's standard for righteous living to be patient because God is not through yet. Funny how patience is something we all tend to desire when we are the recipients but sometimes struggle to extend as quickly and generously to others. Patience is even difficult for many when it comes to the expectations we place on ourselves. Yet perhaps one of the most challenging applications is sufficient patience to wait on God. We are programmed to expect perfection and immediate action. When life throws us a curveball and we find ourselves unexpectedly maneuvering unknown territory, the need to slow down and rely on God takes us out of our comfort zone. We realize not only are we not in control as if that weren't a big enough challenge, but we can't even anticipate what will happen next, how, or when. Romans 5:3 tells us we should glory in these situations because tribulations work patience. Maybe that is why we are cautioned to be careful praying for patience because the answer to that prayer will inevitably cause us to face situations requiring a level of patience we've not known.

Some refer to "the patience of Job" when life requires us to be still and wait on God, especially when friends come to criticize and to blame us for undesired conditions. In such predicaments, our ability to release, to relax, and to refresh become critical to how we move forward. In Job 13:15, we find the declaration, "Though He slay me, yet will I trust in Him." This absolute resolve to remain aligned with God, no matter what, is a strong release of control. In a situation where many would not only lack patience but also find it easy to walk away from God, Job goes further in Job 14:14 to say "…all the days of my appointed time will I wait, till my change come." At this point I picture Job throwing up his hands in total surrender, releasing the situation to God and sitting down to relax since he can't do anything but wait on God. The "patience of Job" will bring us to a place of stress-free living if we can truly release control, and understanding that God is the only One who can bring us through and it is His responsibility to do just that. Once we accept this truth and stop trying to work things out in our own strength, we can actually relax in situations while we wait patiently for God's best outcome in our life. It has been said that it is not enough to wait but the key is in "how" we wait. We can wait grudgingly. We can wait in despair. We can wait patiently. Hebrews 12:2 encourages us to look to Jesus, the Author and Finisher of our faith. When we focus our eyes on Jesus, we can release control and relax while we patiently wait. We can even find ourselves refreshed as we enter into His rest (Hebrews 4:1-11).

A couple we know struggled with marital issues over a number of years. After 12 years of the husband's battle with pornography and other women, the wife discovered he had purchased a vehicle for another woman the prior month and had been paying the lady's rent. Meanwhile, the wife did not have a vehicle to drive. The initial decision after conferring with their pastor was to retrieve the car from the other lady, sell it, and use the proceeds to purchase a vehicle for the wife. Given the years of extreme disappointment and hurt, we could not have guessed what the wife did next. She decided to take the vehicle title to the lady and share Christ with her. She also washed her husband's feet and positioned herself to walk alongside him with the care and sensitivity one would give a baby trying to grow. Not at all what any of us would have expected but truly evidence that her time with God in the wake of this devastating situation yielded fruit only He could produce. As they walked it out, more discoveries of infidelity and lies surfaced week after week. Despite moments of discouragement and wondering what else she might learn, she did not abandon the position of grace toward her husband. Long-suffering? Patience? A powerful example indeed of God's love and grace in action despite the extended seasons of suffering.

The ability to suffer long without complaining is a key indication of the Holy Spirit's work in our lives. Once we master patience with God's plan for our lives and understand how longsuffering He is toward us, we are better positioned to be patient with others. Why? Because God is not finished with any of us. Aren't we grateful!

Patience Prayer for My Sister

Lord, thank You for Your great love and patience for all of us. May my sister become keenly aware of all the ways You've extended patience to her and may she in turn find it easier to be patient with herself, others, and even You. Thank You for carrying her through every situation of life such that her tribulations will indeed work patience in her. May she hold on to Galatians 6:9 and not grow weary in well-doing knowing in due season she will reap a good harvest if she holds on and does not faint in the waiting. In the name of Jesus Christ. Amen.

MIRROR MOMENT

A

AFFECT
(EMOTIONS)

B

BEHAVIOR
(ACTIONS)

C

COGNITION
(THOUGHTS)

~Reflections ~

SOAP BIBLE STUDY METHOD

S - Scripture

Read the scripture without trying to determine meaning. Just read what is there.

O - Observance

Notice what stands out for you or what captures your attention. Sometimes, using the 5 W's helps with this – who, what, when, where, why, and how?

A - Application

Ask yourself, "so what?" How does this apply to me and my life and how can I utilize it in my life?" Be honest with yourself.

P - Prayer

Pray without ceasing. Pray before. Pray during. Pray afterwards. Be prayerful throughout this process.

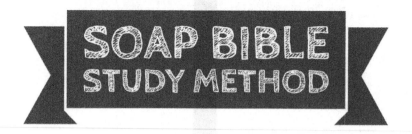

SOAP BIBLE STUDY METHOD

S - Scripture

O - Observance

A - Application

P - Prayer

SCRIPTURES ON THIS FRUIT

SEEDS TO PRODUCE MUCH FRUIT

Compass Points

What action(s) were taken? What action(s) do you need to take?

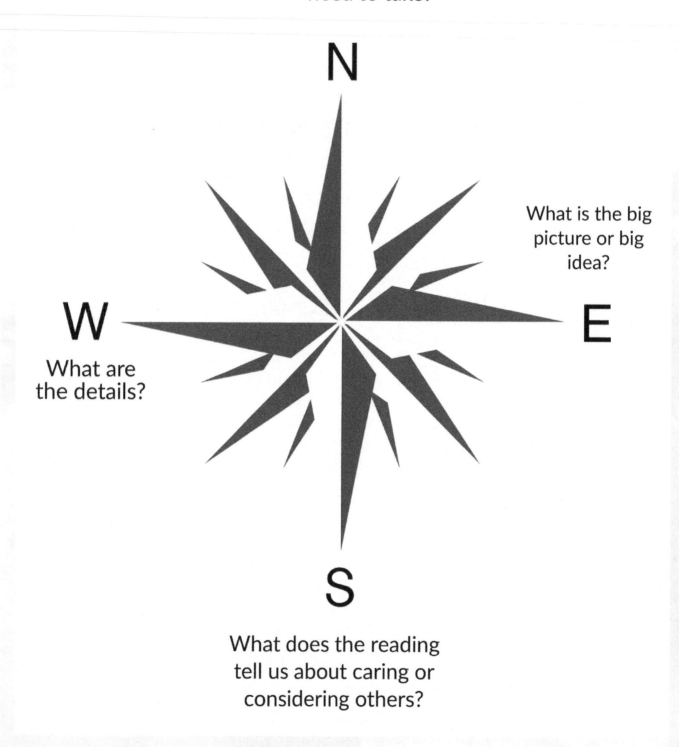

N

E

What is the big picture or big idea?

W

What are the details?

S

What does the reading tell us about caring or considering others?

Note to self

K

What do you know?

W

What do you want to know?

L

What did you learn?

Made in the image of God

Month:

Month:

KINDNESS

PUT ON THEREFORE, AS THE ELECT OF GOD, HOLY AND BELOVED, BOWELS OF MERCIES, KINDNESS, HUMBLENESS OF MIND, MEEKNESS, LONGSUFFERING...

COLOSSIANS 3:12

KINDNESS

PUT ON THEREFORE, AS THE ELECT OF GOD, HOLY AND BELOVED, BOWELS OF MERCIES, KINDNESS, HUMBLENESS OF MIND, MEEKNESS, LONGSUFFERING.

COLOSSIANS 3:12

Kindness

By Kimberly Mucker-Johnson

Colossians 3:12-13 - *Put on therefore, as the elect of God, holy and beloved, bowels of mercies, kindness, humbleness of mind, meekness, longsuffering; 13 Forbearing one another, and forgiving one another, if any man have a quarrel against any: even as Christ forgave you, so also do ye.*

I remember so vividly when I was a young child in school, we would have to come up with an adjective that began with the same letter as our first name. My first name is Kimberly, so there aren't that many "k" adjectives to choose from (not that I knew of, anyway), so I would always choose "kind"... Kind Kimberly. At the time, I didn't know what kindness really meant and even before completing this project, I still did not have a true understanding of it. I would say I thought like everyone else that kindness meant to be nice or to do something for someone. **NOW I KNOW!!**

I looked up the word kindness using online dictionaries, and I discovered that kindness was synonymous with words such as friendliness, generous, sympathetic, merciful, empathetic, or understanding. However, what was new to me was the word origin for kindness. Apparently, kindness was originally the word "kyndnes". Kyndnes comes from Old English and it means nation, produce, and increase. So, I was confused as to how this word started off meaning nation, produce, and increase, and then later meant friendliness, generous, sympathetic, etc. This led me to turn to the Bible for clarification and to find out what thus said the Lord on this topic. First, I looked up the meaning of nation in the Bible. Nation means all people. We are all made in the image of God. We are all brothers and sisters in the Lord. We are all kin, which is the little word inside of the word "kindness". Next, I looked up kindness in the Bible, and it was always associated with family members or kinfolk showing mercy, grace, selflessness, compassion, etc. What is even more powerful about kindness is that it produces increase when it is shown to your enemies and the "least among you".

This new knowledge of kindness required me to study it even more. I discovered that kindness is a choice. The scripture clearly tells us to put on (like an outfit or your best dress) "bowels (large amount) of mercy, kindness, humbleness of mind, meekness, and longsuffering (to suffer long)" (Colossians 3:12). For this is evidence of the forbearing and forgiving that are mentioned in verse 13. And to take off (the outfit that doesn't look right or doesn't fit right or just isn't right for you) "..anger, wrath, malice, blasphemy, filthy communication out of your mouth. Lie not one to another, seeing that ye have put off the old man with his deeds" (Colossians 3:8-9).

Remember, kindness is not always easy. Therefore, you will need to pray without ceasing because the choice of kindness or the unconditional yes of kindness will always cost you something. Yeah, I get it! We don't have "money" to keep paying or "it's too expensive". Well, first of all, it's not your money. You are to be a good steward of the Lord's vineyard.

Next, when you pay in kindness, then you will reap in kindness. ***YOU CANNOT BEAT GOD GIVING!!*** I remember one time I was in my probationary period at a new job (90 days), and it was unbearingly hot outside. I went to the bank during my lunch period (30 minutes). At the bank, I met this 90-something year old woman. She looked as if she was going to just faint from the extreme weather. I feared for her safety as I watched her struggle to walk to the bus stop. She just seemed so frail, and all I could think of was if this was someone in my family would I want them on a bus stop and to potentially faint in this extreme heat. I knew the consequences of me not coming back from lunch on time. I knew it could cost me my job. There was no use in calling and trying to explain this situation because even I didn't understand the test that was before me. Ultimately, after a struggle with myself against myself, the part of me that had to show this woman some kindness won over the part of me that said I was about to lose my new job. I asked the lady if she needed a ride. She told me yes. She lived deep in the west end and we were downtown (my job was in the south central part of the city). She was barely able to get into the car. The whole time I felt bad for her but she managed to get into the care. As I was driving, I asked her if she needed anything else. She stated that she needed to pick up her medication from the pharmacy. One part of me was saying out loud, "That's not a problem. We'll stop at the pharmacy." The other part of me, that was speaking internally, was like, "You don't have time for all of this. This is getting worse and worse. What are you going to do? Eric just married you with two children and now you are getting ready to be unemployed. Really???!!" I made the stops necessary for the woman to get her medication, and then I drove her home. I remember it seemed to take forever for her to get out of the car and walk up to her house and get inside. I remember rushing back to work afterwards. I had probably been gone for an hour and half (at least). I remember my boss did not ask me any questions about what had happened (she did not care). I was immediately ushered to Human Resources where they broke the news to me that I had lost my job, and during the probation period, they did not have to give me a reason. I was hurt as I kept thinking *but I had been kind. I did what God wanted me to do.* Newsflash: Just because you do what God wants you to do...does not mean that it won't cost you something. But do know God will take care of you when you do His will. I remember telling my husband that I had lost my job. Also, I remember never having an opportunity to file for unemployment before I found another job. I don't think I was unemployed a whole week. My kindness was worth it because it was what God wanted me to do. If I had to do it all over again, then I wouldn't change a thing. The part of me that wanted to be good won that day. KINDNESS won!!

Another example of God's work of kindness in me was when one of my jobs required that I advocate for students and families - who were our clients. Advocate means to stand in proxy or intercede on someone's behalf. I started to notice that everytime I mentioned some injustice that was happening to a student and/or family, then I was treated with extreme unkindness by my boss. Although I was being treated this way, I still had to trust the Lord and maintain kindness. It wasn't easy to maintain kindness when others were being unkind. In fact, it was extremely difficult - almost heart-wrenching! People who witnessed what was happening said they did not know how I was doing it. Well, it wasn't me. It was the Lord. I never spoke to my boss disrespectfully, and I constantly tried to do things to make the school better and make her work easier. Eventually, after making up lies on me and falsifying evaluations, etc., she fell ill. This was not a regular illness but it was an extreme illness - to the point that months later, she admitted that she probably had Covid-19. While she was out, I had to do her duties and my own duties. I remember praying for her by text message. I wrote, "I'm sending up many prayers for you. I speak total recovery of your health over you. Right now in the name of Jesus Christ. Amen." She wrote back, "Lol! Thank you." At the time, I kept thinking this is not a joke. My prayers are not a joke because I really seriously wanted her to fully recover. She fully recovered and continued her mission of treating me unkind. I was shocked. I wanted to tell her off and tell her how I had done nothing to her but be kind. But God would not allow me. God taught me to be quiet, and he allowed her to be evil towards me. It was a WAR internally, externally, all over me. I was losing. I knew that when you hold your emotions and feelings inside, then you could possibly implode (that's exploding on the inside). But God kept me. I made it through to the other side. Now, I can look back on that situation and I know that I did the will of God in spite of myself. I did the will of God even though I didn't want to. Finally, I did the will of God and I WON. Victory is mine.

The National Random Acts of Kindness week is usually celebrated in mid-February of every year. However, God is calling His saints to exercise kindness always.

Kindness Prayer for My Sister

Father, in the name of Jesus Christ, I humbly come before you for the person that has just read about kindness and what you said regarding this fruit of the Spirit. Lord, you said that if we need anything that we could come to you and ask. We are asking that you will make us kind towards others. Not just people that we know and love, but help us to be kind to people that are unkind towards us. Help us to be kind to those that could never repay us in any way, shape, or form. Help us to be kind to our enemies and our frenemies. Lord, we now know and understand that kindness is a choice, but Lord, we are also aware of our humanity, which prevents us from sometimes having a desire to choose kindness. Lord, we humbly ask you to put that desire in us and no matter what it looks like - job, losing, etc., let us choose to be kind as our perfect model, Jesus Christ was always kind. Lord, we ask if there are any unrepentant acts of unkindness in us that you will reveal them and enable us to have a mind to repent of those things. Lord, we trust and believe you. Amen.

MIRROR MOMENT

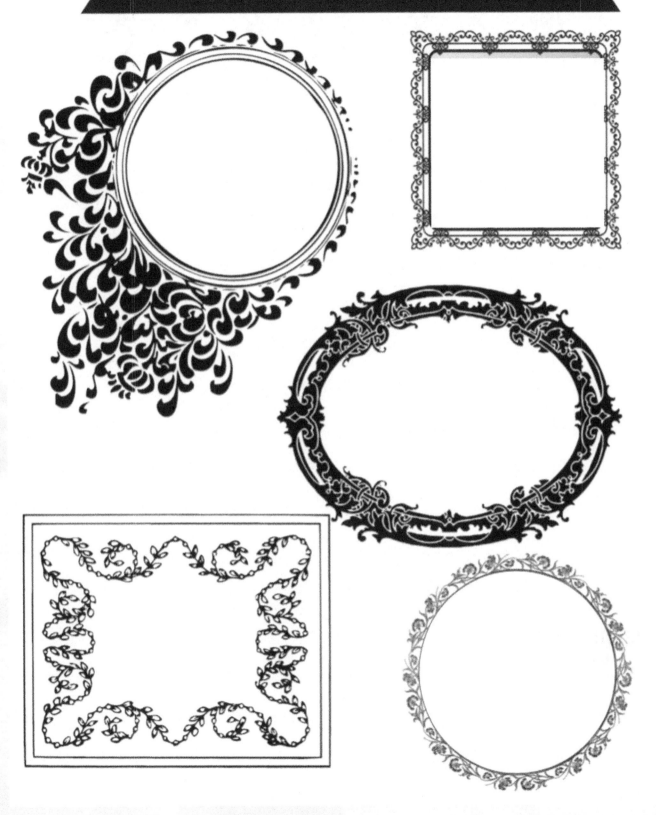

A
AFFECT
(EMOTIONS)

B
BEHAVIOR
(ACTIONS)

C
COGNITION
(THOUGHTS)

~Reflections ~

SOAP BIBLE STUDY METHOD

S - Scripture

Read the scripture without trying to determine meaning. Just read what is there.

O - Observance

Notice what stands out for you or what captures your attention. Sometimes, using the 5 W's helps with this - who, what, when, where, why, and how?

A - Application

Ask yourself, "so what?" How does this apply to me and my life and how can I utilize it in my life?" Be honest with yourself.

P - Prayer

Pray without ceasing. Pray before. Pray during. Pray afterwards. Be prayerful throughout this process.

SOAP BIBLE STUDY METHOD

S - Scripture   O - Observance

A - Application   P - Prayer

SCRIPTURES ON THIS FRUIT

SEEDS TO PRODUCE MUCH FRUIT

Compass Points

What action(s) were taken? What action(s) do you need to take?

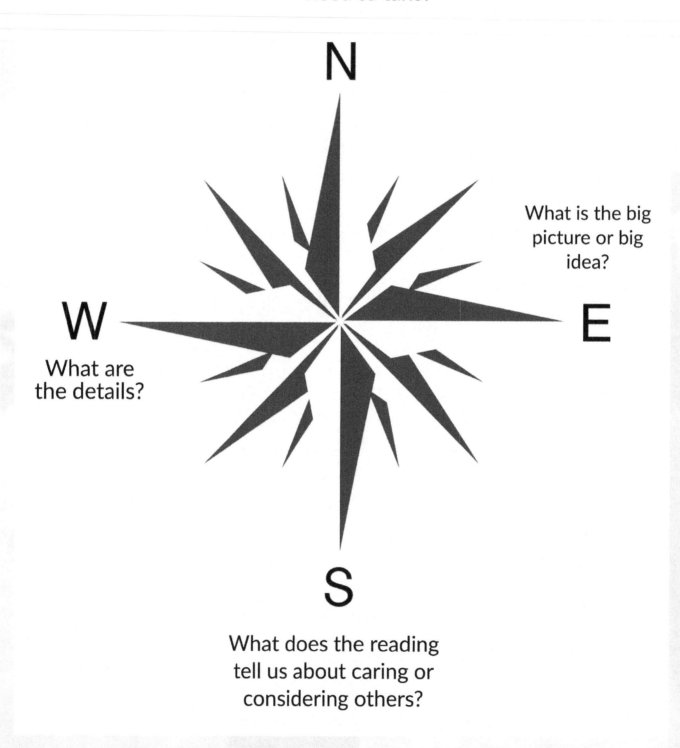

N

What is the big picture or big idea?

E

W

What are the details?

S

What does the reading tell us about caring or considering others?

Note to self

K
What do you know?

W
What do you want to know?

L
What did you learn?

Made in the image of God

Month:

KINDNESS

Month:

KINDNESS

GOODNESS

OH TASTE AND SEE THAT THE LORD IS GOOD! – PSALM 34:8

GOODNESS

OH TASTE AND SEE THAT THE LORD IS GOOD! – PSALM 34:8

Goodness
By Mechelle Roberson

As I sit here, I have transported myself back to those days. You are probably wondering, what days I am talking about? I am talking about the days when praise and worship consisted of testimony time. I remember hearing the organ as I walked swiftly across the parking lot. I knew what time it was. It was testimony service. Do you remember testimony service? Wow! It was explosive with the power of God! It was a time for God's people to share His goodness unto them. A moment to be uplifted by people's experiences. It was a magnificent time in the Lord. The songs the old mothers of the church sung would bolt the atmosphere. Songs like, "When I think of the goodness of Jesus and all He has done for me; my soul cries out Hallelujah, I praise God for saving me". Another mother of the church would say "You know, God has been good to me, He woke me up this morning with the activity of my limbs and gave me a sound mind". One testimony after another exclaiming the goodness of God. By this time, the atmosphere was charged with His goodness. You could not help but to weep, rock side to side, raise your hands, magnify Him, and shout hallelujah all the while thinking about what He has done in your life. You would feel rejuvenated and empowered to face the challenges of the enemy for the upcoming week. Oh, how I miss testimony service! The Word of God states, "And they overcame….by the word of their testimony… (Revelation 12:11). There is life and death in the power of the tongue (Proverbs 18:21). The enemy knows your mouth can kill his plans. Plans he has devised to take you out. This is why he tries to shut your mouth. He does not want you to share the goodness of God. The more we exclaim His mighty works, the more faith becomes manifested in our lives. You began to believe in His goodness.

What is goodness? The goodness of God consists of righteousness, kind-heartedness, lovingness, compassion, excellence, tolerance, patience, fairness, graciousness, and tender-heartedness. Genesis chapter one details the creation of God and it was good. Everything God does is GOOD! Mark 7:37 states, "…He does all things well." God is good! I got a testimony! At the age of sixteen, I was diagnosed with Polycystic Ovary Syndrome (PCOS). It is a hormonal disorder common among women of childbearing age. It can affect your ability to have a child or as your doctor will call it, "your fertility". The doctor suggested I began birth control to regulate my menstrual cycle which I took for twelve years. Initially, it did not resonate with me the difficulties I could have in conceiving. I was only sixteen at the time of the diagnosis. As I got older, I did wonder about the "what if's". What if I cannot conceive on my own? What if I cannot have children? Then I remembered the doctor saying we have medication that can help you conceive when the time comes. Well, the time came! I got married at twenty-eight years old. Did you do the math? It was twelve years later. My husband and I were leaving Wednesday night prayer. We had been married for approximately two months. He leans over in the car and says, "I heard the Lord say, you should stop taking the pills". I was shocked and asked when did he hear that. He said while we were at prayer service. I said, okay. I was not concerned because I had been told in the past that it takes months for the birth control to get out of your system. Remember, it had been twelve years. I thought it would be a while before I would conceive. Do not judge me. I get it, you are probably wondering how a believer can rely on a doctor's report. Well, I would too. I relied on the doctor's report. I was young in God. My faith was small. To be honest, I failed to remember His goodness unto me. I know now that I will believe the report of the Lord. Doctors give a diagnosis, but it does not define who we are in God. God is a healer! Praise God! Hallelujah! A few weeks later, I decided to schedule a doctor's appointment with my OBGYN to discuss my options for conception. My mother went with me because my husband had to work. The doctor went over my options and asked if we had any questions. Of course, my mother would (the healthcare worker). They say healthcare workers are the worst patients. Although she was not the patient, I was, and that was enough for her to ask questions. There is nothing like a mother advocating for her child. My mother asked, could she be pregnant now? The doctor adamantly said no. My mother was sure I was pregnant and suggested they give me a pregnancy test. My doctor ordered the test and said they would call me with the results. I received the phone call later that afternoon from my doctor. She wanted to personally call me. I remember like it was yesterday. I can hear her laughter as she told me I was pregnant. She really could not believe I did not need help. She congratulated me with laughter flowing from her words. I was shocked. We had only been married for approximately two months and I was already pregnant. God is truly a miracle worker! I did not doubt He would do the unthinkable, just not within two months of marriage. Well, we were excited! My mother was right. A mother knows her child even if the child is an adult! I pray this testimony speaks to your situation. God can do anything! He is simply amazing!

Whatever you are facing this moment, remember you serve a Big God! He is greater and mightier than your problem. I compel you to reach out and touch Him. How? Touch Him through your praise, worship, and prayer. He sees the dilemma you are facing and wants to help you. Tell Him about what He has done for others and you know He can do that for you. Remind Him who He is in your life. Give Him the accolades He is due. He will see about you! I promise! He loves you just like He loves me. God does not have favorites. We that are baptized in the Holy Spirit are His children. He wants you to prosper and be in good health. (III John 1:2) I am a witness to what God can do. Oh, I failed to mention, I (we) had a son. God continued to bless us with two more sons without any assistance from a physician. Well, the Chief Physician did it. That is Jesus Christ! He is worthy to be praised. There is a balm in Gilead! What is this balm? It is herbs and spices that served as a healing ointment used to heal or soothe the skin and was contained in Gilead (an area east of the Jordan river). The metaphorical phrase "Jesus is a balm" is used to describe the healing power of Jesus. He brings healing for the body, soul, mind, and spirit. I needed physical healing. He regulated my reproduction system. He is the balm! What a miraculous God we serve!

Goodness Prayer for My Sister

Let us pray together. Lord Jesus, I believe in Your Word. I will believe Your report that says You are a healer. Lord Jesus, please help my unbelief. Help me to trust Your plan for my life. Your purpose will prevail! I thank you for the blessings you have already given. But, Lord, I need one right now. Please shower Your goodness upon me. Let me feel your presence. I want to experience Your loving kindness which is better than life. Help me to reflect on Your goodness. You displayed Your goodness unto me before I was conceived in my mother's womb. You established me for Your Kingdom. That is why I am fearfully and wonderfully made. I know if I reflect on Your goodness my faith will be increased. I will testify to myself Your goodness and mercy unto me. I am an overcomer. I thank You for all You have done, and I am excited to see what You are going to do next. I will praise You forever. I will testify to the world of Your goodness unto me. In Jesus Name Amen!

GOODNESS

OH TASTE AND SEE THAT THE LORD IS GOOD! - PSALM 34:8

MIRROR MOMENT

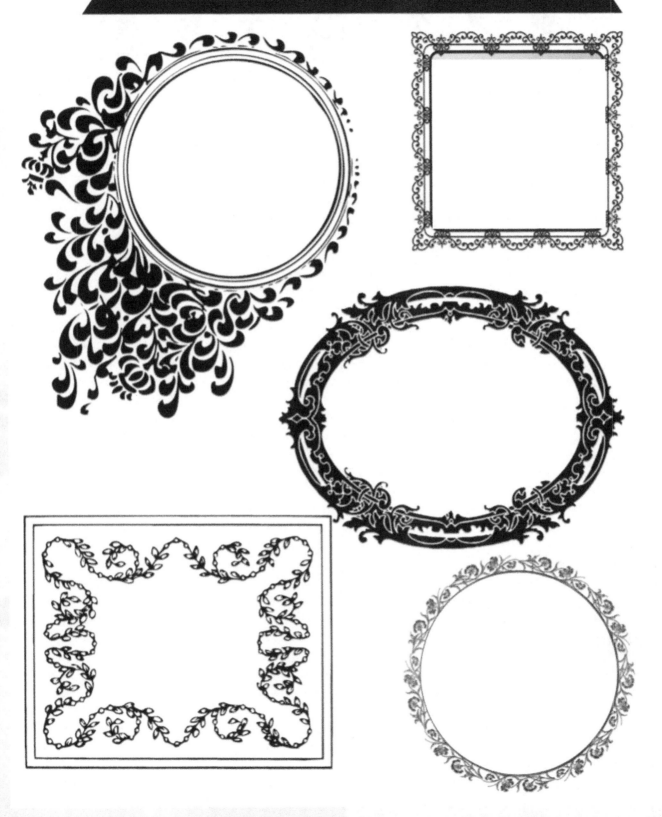

A
AFFECT
(EMOTIONS)

B
BEHAVIOR
(ACTIONS)

C
COGNITION
(THOUGHTS)

~Reflections ~

SOAP BIBLE STUDY METHOD

S - Scripture

Read the scripture without trying to determine meaning. Just read what is there.

O - Observance

Notice what stands out for you or what captures your attention. Sometimes, using the 5 W's helps with this – who, what, when, where, why, and how?

A - Application

Ask yourself, "so what?" How does this apply to me and my life and how can I utilize it in my life?" Be honest with yourself.

P - Prayer

Pray without ceasing. Pray before. Pray during. Pray afterwards. Be prayerful throughout this process.

SOAP BIBLE STUDY METHOD

S - Scripture   O - Observance

A - Application   P - Prayer

SCRIPTURES ON THIS FRUIT

SEEDS TO PRODUCE MUCH FRUIT

Compass Points

What action(s) were taken? What action(s) do you need to take?

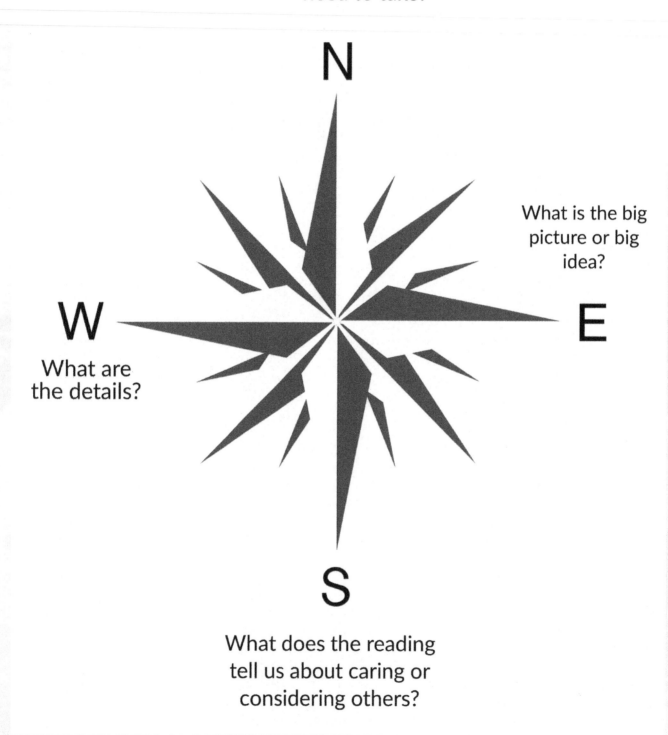

N

What is the big picture or big idea?

W

E

What are the details?

S

What does the reading tell us about caring or considering others?

Note to self

K
What do you know?

W
What do you want to know?

L
What did you learn?

Made in the image of God

Month:

Month:

GOODNESS

OH

Faithfulness

IT IS OF THE LORD'S MERCIES THAT WE ARE NOT CONSUMED, BECAUSE HIS COMPASSIONS FAIL NOT. THEY ARE NEW EVERY MORNING: GREAT IS THY FAITHFULNESS. LAMENTATIONS 3:22-23

Faithfulness

IT IS OF THE LORD'S MERCIES THAT WE ARE NOT CONSUMED, BECAUSE HIS COMPASSIONS FAIL NOT. THEY ARE NEW EVERY MORNING: GREAT IS THY FAITHFULNESS. LAMENTATIONS 3:22-23

Faithfulness

By Mechelle Roberson

For God says, **"Your cry came to me at a favorable time, when the doors of welcome were wide open. I helped you on a day when salvation was being offered"** *(2 Corinthians 6:2, Living Bible). Right now, God is ready to welcome you. Today he is ready to save you.*

Can you think of something that is constant in your life? Is there something you can rely on to be true? What do you depend upon daily? Do you trust it will never change? Would you consider it to be on your loyal list?

Are you ready to take this journey with me? I hope you do not mind, but I chose the beach for our talk. I love connecting with nature and enjoying God's creation. Additionally, it is peaceful and calming. Did you know there are over 300 species of birds that live near the ocean? I am sure we will enjoy their melodious singing as well. I just think it is a perfect setting to discuss the fruit of the spirit, specifically, FAITHFULNESS. I am expecting God to broaden our horizon, empower and inspire us. Let us begin!

According to New World Encyclopedia, **"faith"** (from Greek-*pistis* and Latin-*fides*) refers to confidence, trust, and hope in God, a person, community, tradition, or locus of inspiration". Based on my research, faithfulness and favorable are semantically related. Meaning, both can be used interchangeably. For our discussion, I will use faithfulness more than favorable. Faithfulness is the characteristic of God's ethical nature. It is a quality related to both God and man. Faithfulness is comparable to the words unchangeable, loyal, and constant. The faithfulness of God is His steadfast commitment to keeping His promises to us. His Word will not return unto Him void (Isaiah 55:11). There are three examples of faithfulness that I will share. The first one is relevant today and the other two are examples from the Word of God. The first example of faithfulness is the loyalty of a man's best friend, his dog. He is always by his side. The second example of faithfulness is from the Bible. Ruth's commitment to serving her mother-in-law, Naomi, which yielded a great reward. She is in the lineage of our Lord and Savior Jesus Christ. The third example is God's promise to give Sarah and Abraham a son in their old age and establish an everlasting covenant with him and his descendants. A few key words of faithfulness to keep in mind are trust, committed, loyal, promise and constancy.

I am sure you can tell time, right? Me too. I was taught in kindergarten or first grade, I believe. You remember, the big hand-little hand. Seems so easy to control that kind of time. If your device is not working properly, then you simply change the battery. It is difficult to tell time in the dark. Some watches have a button on the side of the watch to activate the light (if you have a fancy-dandy kind). Wow, what about the watch that glows in the dark. I have one of those. My husband bought one for me on my 40th birthday. Geez, that has been a minute. SMILE! As a matter of fact, it is a citizen brand. In the dark, the face changes to a soft and radiant mother of pearl (pinkish color). The Citizen brand is classic, reliable, inexpensive, enduring and has been around since 1930. I expect the time to be accurate when I put it on. No matter the geographical area, I expect the time to be correct on my device. Did you know there are seven time zones in the United States of America? Well, it is true. I looked up the time zones in the United States of America and discovered there were seven. From east to west, they are Atlantic Standard Time (AST), Eastern Standard Time (EST), Central Standard Time (CST), Mountain Standard Time (MST), Pacific Standard Time (PST), Alaskan Standard Time (AKST), Hawaii-Aleutian Standard Time (HST), Samoa standard time (UTC-11) and Chamorro Standard Time (UTC+10). Depending upon the geographical area you live in, you expect your device to give the correct time. This time is expected because it has been set to one of the above time zones. Again, you rely on the device to provide the correct time.

Well, there is a time you cannot set or predict. The time that God will move on your behalf; The time of His coming. We know He is going to answer our call. But, when! What will He say? Only time will reveal His majestic work. I have been asking God for a memo for an exceptionally long time. I promised Him I would follow the bullet points. SMILE! I have not received one yet. It would probably overwhelm me. Yes, I want to know His plan. But the expectation of the outcome or where I stand in the plan would be exhausting. I over analyze everything. Bless my heart! Geez! I am a solutionist, so I walk into a situation with my antennas tuned in and ready to resolve the problem. One would think by now I would relinquish the desire to resolve the problem. The Word of God assures me "with Him all things are possible" (Matthew 19:26). There are thirteen verses in the Bible that references this very fact. I choose not to doubt His Word but rely on His faithfulness.

Approximately three years ago, life happened! Keep living, life will visit you. But there is nothing too hard for God (Jeremiah

32:27). Hindsight is 20/20, it was time for me to let go. Let go of the rigid, tensed, too focused and principled- oriented me. Whew, I needed a transformation. I had no idea the package would be wrapped and delivered in this manner. Not pretty! It was delivered unexpectedly. I needed the result of the package, but I must admit I would not have chosen the contents. It was January 2017, my mother's brother passed away and we were preparing to drive to Jackson, Tennessee. It was a terribly busy time at work, plus the environment was hostile. I was wrapping up the month end so we could leave early to get on the road and navigate home life. You know, work-life balance, it is no joke. At the time, we had three sons in school and that presented more challenges. We were financially strapped which added more layers. In summation, I was overwhelmed, exhausted and depleted! I thought I was releasing my challenges in prayer and venting to my sisters/friends. It was not enough!

My mom and I got on the road to Jackson, TN. It was my turn to drive. I had been drinking a diet coke and eating M&Ms for the caffeine boost. Approximately 15 minutes in, I began to feel dizzy and fuzzy. Not good! I told my mom, "I can't drive". So, I pulled over to the emergency lane and she took over. We continued the journey, and I began to feel worse. My mom asked what my symptoms were. I told her I felt dizzy, fuzzy, and felt like my legs were vibrating. This was the only description I could give. I knew it sounded incomprehensible, but this is what my body was going through. I became concerned. I had never experienced anything like this. Of course, my mother was concerned, yet she remained prayerful. We made it to the hotel, checked in and got situated in our room. I began to feel somewhat better, not much. The symptoms were coming and going. Sadly, I was not able to attend the funeral and be with my loved ones. I was disappointed, but at the same time desired to be well. I stayed behind and rested. Again, feeling better and I knew the next day would be much better. Well, my next day was not the same timing as God's next day. On our way back home the following day, we stopped at a Walgreens to check my blood pressure. It was high, mainly due to the discomfort my body was experiencing. We began to travel home. I was not in pain, just an unexplainable discomfort that became difficult to explain. After visiting the ER via the ambulance, we finally made it home. My mom was prayerful, but extremely concerned. I am her only child, so that was to be expected.

On January 8, 2017, I saw my primary physician. I began to share what happened. She diagnosed me with stress and handed me a prescription for blood pressure and anxiety medicine. I became highly upset. Me, stress, and anxiety. Absolutely not! I thought, she does not know what she is talking about. I took the blood pressure medicine, but I refused to take the anxiety medicine. The symptoms remained. My friends and family had their opinions about the medicines and diagnosis. I began to feel no one has a clue what I am dealing with. This is scary! It was the unknown about the origin of my symptoms that startled me. It got worse before it got better. I eventually took the anxiety medicine. I felt ashamed, defeated, and lost.

The next phase was challenging. I began watching TBN (Trinity Broadcasting Network) Christian television and reading the Word of God. I memorized two main passages of the Bible and quoted throughout the day. For God hath not given us the spirit of fear; but of power, and of love, and of a sound mind. (2 Timothy 1:7 KJV) and I shall not die, but live, and declare the works of the Lord (Psalm 118:1 KJV). The Word and Prayer were my saving grace. On March 15, 2017, I wrote in the back of my bible "This will not last.

God began to guide me to which specialist to see. I was walking in obedience and faith. The next six or eight weeks included me seeing multiple specialists, many medical tests, in and out from work, not able to drive, multiple 911 calls/ER visits, no help around the house and losing approximately 40 lbs. I saw four specialists which were a cardiologist, gastroenterologist, ear nose and throat and finally an allergist. The gastroenterologist found polyps that were not cancerous. Praise God! Had I not gone, I would not have known they were lying inside my body.

The last specialist was the allergist. I told the allergy doctor I needed a food allergy test. Funny, we self-diagnose and order our own method of treatment. He said, "you do not need an allergy test, you do not have food allergy. You have silent reflux". The medical term is laryngopharyngeal reflux. Who knew! I began to cry when he confirmed I was not losing it. I felt alone! I did not doubt I was under extreme pressure from my home and work life. However, I knew it was something more I was up against. He gave me several medicines to help with the SILENT REFLUX. Seems to me it made a lot of noise. LOL!

The journey to recovery was challenging. There were many emotions I had to overcome such as doubt and fear. I was literally transforming in the midst of recovery. See, this package delivered a necessary change in my life. It had to take place. I desired to be more like God. I did not know I would find Him, know Him greater, trust Him more and obey His commands in the midst of being broken. He heard me crying. Each tear drop, He knew! He was faithful concerning His promises. He delivered me in the nick of time! He did not leave nor forsake me! This timing could not be set, predicted, or altered. The transformation had to take place in my life for the destiny he has prepared for me. God could have delivered a different package. He could have cancelled the delivery. But He did not! I had to accept the process. It was tough! It was lonely! His grace was sufficient (2 Corinthians 12:9). I knew God was coming to my rescue. I did not know the timing of His coming. Again, He was faithful and on time. To God be the Glory!

Faithfulness Prayer for My Sister

Lord, I thank You for the wonderful many blessings You have bestowed upon us. Because Your lovingkindness is better than life; my lips will give You praise. I come on behalf of the readers of this journal. Please help the women who are struggling with trusting Your Word. I pray they have a greater understanding and appreciation for Your timing. You do all things well. You are never late. We are grateful that You answer our call when we cry unto You. Lord, we thank You for Your faithfulness. You have delivered time and time again. Your Word will not return unto You void. We will forever be grateful for the covenant that You have made with Your people. Lord, we ask that You help our unbelief. Help us to be faithful concerning the calling and gifting You have placed upon us. Lord, we need more constancy and trust in our lives. So many have been wounded on the battlefield and not sure who they can rely on. Lord Jesus, heal and deliver Your people. Lord, I pray every woman that reads this journal succumbs to Your love, commands and will. Lord Jesus, I pray a burning desire to grow closer to You takes residence in their hearts. We know it is "in the dwelling" where we grow to know You more. I thank You in advance for all You are going to do on our behalf. In Jesus' name Amen!

Faithfulness

IT IS OF THE LORD'S MERCIES THAT WE ARE NOT CONSUMED,
BECAUSE HIS COMPASSIONS FAIL NOT. THEY ARE NEW EVERY MORNING:
GREAT IS THY FAITHFULNESS. LAMENTATIONS 3:22-23

MIRROR MOMENT

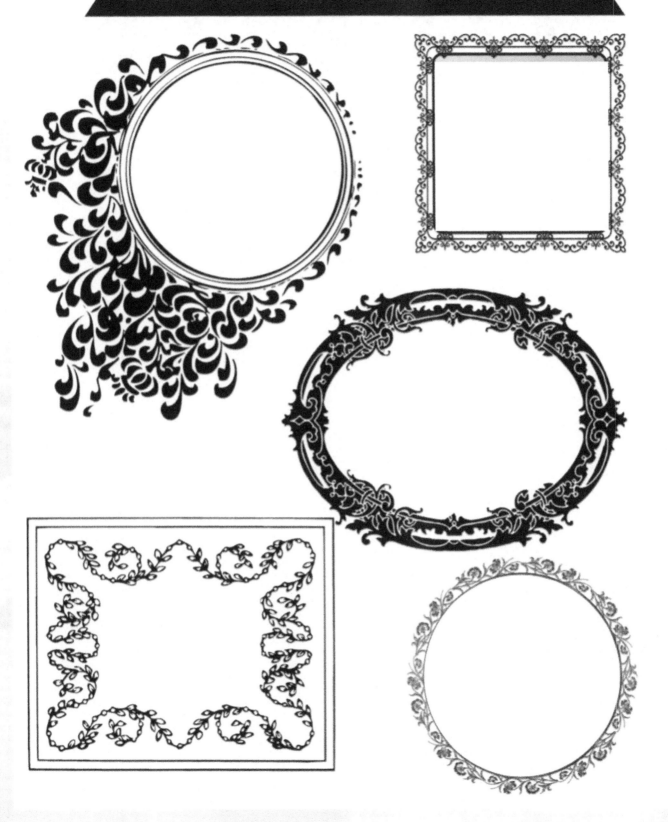

A — AFFECT (EMOTIONS)

B — BEHAVIOR (ACTIONS)

C — COGNITION (THOUGHTS)

~Reflections~

SOAP BIBLE STUDY METHOD

S - Scripture

Read the scripture without trying to determine meaning. Just read what is there.

O - Observance

Notice what stands out for you or what captures your attention. Sometimes, using the 5 W's helps with this - who, what, when, where, why, and how?

A - Application

Ask yourself, "so what?" How does this apply to me and my life and how can I utilize it in my life?" Be honest with yourself.

P - Prayer

Pray without ceasing. Pray before. Pray during. Pray afterwards. Be prayerful throughout this process.

SOAP BIBLE STUDY METHOD

S - Scripture   O - Observance

A - Application   P - Prayer

SCRIPTURES ON THIS FRUIT

SEEDS TO PRODUCE MUCH FRUIT

Compass Points

What action(s) were taken? What action(s) do you need to take?

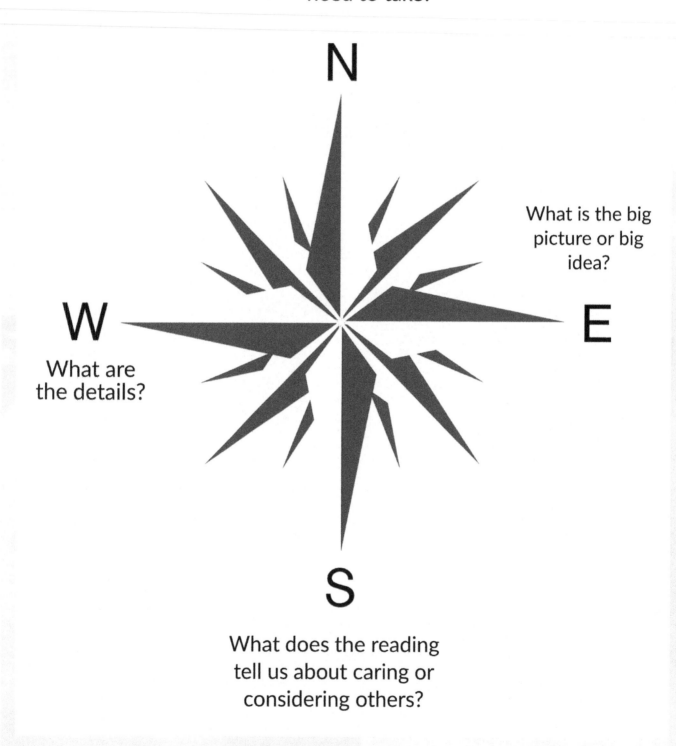

N

W

What are
the details?

What is the big
picture or big
idea?

E

S

What does the reading
tell us about caring or
considering others?

Note to self

K

What do you know?

W

What do you want to know?

L

What did you learn?

Made in the image of God

136

Month:

IT I   IED,
BEC   ING:
GR   -23

Month:

Psalm 18:35

GENTLENESS

Psalm 18:35

GENTLENESS

Gentleness

By Kimberly Mucker-Johnson

We all have experienced the physical state of gentleness. It could've been that you've held a newborn baby's face close to your face, or you felt the gentle wind blow across your face. Or maybe you've experienced the still, calm voice of the Lord. We may not be able to describe gentleness with the right words or in ways that make sense to others, but we all know gentleness when we experience it. We know gentleness in the natural. But what about the action of gentleness. What about the fruit of the Spirit called gentleness.

"That's why I take pleasure in my weaknesses, and in the insults, hardships, persecutions, and troubles that I suffer for Christ. For when I am weak, then I am strong" (2 Corinthians 12:10). We learn in the scriptures that God's thoughts and ways are above anything that we can think or do (Isaiah 55:8, 9). There is no exception to this fact when we consider gentleness. Many people think that gentleness means to be weak, to be tame, or to have a deficiency in courage; however, in the Bible, the examples of gentleness also translated as meekness, show us that this word is "power under control". In the Old Testament, Moses was described as the meekest man on earth (Numbers 12:3). Jesus tells us in Matthew 11:28-29, "Come unto me, all ye that labour and are heavy laden, and I will give you rest. Take my yoke upon you and learn of me; for I am meek and lowly in heart: and ye shall find rest unto your souls." In these two examples, it is clear that "meekness," does NOT mean weakness. Gentleness requires great strength and self-control. In fact, *Prautes*, the Greek word for "gentleness" means "to submit one's strength in a posture of humility. This "power under control" means we refuse to inflate and assert ourselves above others. Paul captures this in Romans 12:3. "For by the grace given to me I say to everyone among you not to think of yourself more highly than you ought to think, but to think with sober judgment, each according to the measure of faith that God has assigned." Being gentle requires you to surrender self in order to be a servant of God -to have a servant's heart. In fact, one way to recognize when you or someone else is not being gentle is the manifestation of pride, anger, or revenge.

One of my favorite examples of gentleness is in John 8. A woman "taken in adultery, in the very act" is at the center of this story as the Pharisees quote the Law of Moses, which stated that she was to be executed by stoning. After quoting this Law, they asked Jesus for his opinion on this situation. Jesus stooped down and used his finger to write something on the ground as if he did not hear the Pharisees. In my years of hearing this particular text taught by various teachers, there has been much speculation about what Jesus wrote on the ground. But while writing this, I find myself intrigued with the fact that Jesus stooped. There are two main definitions for stooping. The first definition has to do with bending or kneeling your body. The second one can be perceived as negative. It has to do with lowering your moral standards to the point of doing something reprehensible. This word reprehensible has so many synonyms: deplorable, disgraceful, despicable, shameful, dishonorable, unpardonable, inexcusable, blameworthy, etc. In studying this text, I can see how Jesus was acting out the first definition of kneeling. To me, when Jesus stooped, he kneeled to the will of the Father while at the same time, he became our shame, so he displayed both definitions at the same time. He voluntarily took our dishonor onto himself. He became deplorable so that we could be free. He became blameworthy, so we can be blameless. The tears streaming down my face right now are not tears of sorrow, but they are indeed tears of joy. Gentleness is strength, humility, and self-sacrifice. The Pharisees continued to ask Jesus, "What do you say?" Finally, Jesus stood up and said, "He that is without sin among you, let him first cast a stone at her" (John 8:7). Jesus was not weak nor passive. He stood up to them for her. Then, he stooped down and continued writing. They left one by one starting with the oldest to the youngest as they were each convicted in their own conscience. Jesus did not condemn the woman but he was gentle. He told her, "Go, and sin no more." Just as Jesus was gentle with the woman in this story, God is gentle with us. Even in our sin, He continues to love us. He does not keep record of our wrongs, but offers forgiveness if we come to Him. Jesus wants us to be gentle to others. Matthew 6:14-15 says, "For if you forgive other people when they sin against you, your heavenly Father will also forgive you. But if you do not forgive others their sins, your Father will not forgive your sins."

As an educator, I have to constantly work with various people. There have been so many times when parents have come to the school to talk to me about their child's education. Often, they are angry for various reasons. Over the years as I have matured in Christ, I've learned that when people are frustrated and angry it often has nothing to do with me. It is often not personal. Sometimes, the parent is fed up with his/her child and just doesn't know what else to do. Or they may have taken off work to come to the school and are feeling the stress of that. Or it could just be the stressors associated with life itself. So, I always make sure that I do not return negative energy when I am getting negative energy. I usually start the conversation off with, "Ms. _____, I appreciate you for coming in" (even if the person is younger than me, I answer with "Yes, ma'am" or "No, ma'am". This seems to always put them at ease. It seems to indicate to them that this woman is being respectful, so I'm going to calm down - a soft answer turns away wrath). I usually end up gaining an ally as we determine ways to meet the needs of his/her child. However, not all situations go this smooth. There have been cases where I have been "gentle", and I do not receive gentleness in return. In those cases, when I feel myself becoming anxious, frustrated, or even angry, I say a quick prayer, which includes honestly telling the Lord how I am feeling (He knows already). Then, my prayers lead to me asking for help. The Lord is faithful to answer this prayer because he knows my motives are pure. He knows I am sincerely acknowledging my humanity, and I need Him.

We know that strength requires a lot of physical or mental effort to continue in the midst of pain - even unbearable pain. The choice of gentleness requires strength or power under control. Being gentle can be unbearably painful. That's why you will not be able to be gentle in all circumstances using your own strength. Gentleness requires the strength of the Lord. Gentleness breeds peace, calm, and consistency of character. It is not volatile or abrupt or puffed up in its response to an ungentle world. There is nothing strong about losing your temper, resorting to aggression, or murdering others through words and actions. In fact, this sort of behavior makes you weak.

Gentleness in practice looks like love, grace, helpfulness, and kindness. Here's a list of ways to add gentleness to your life:

- **Gentleness esteems others above yourself** (Philippians 2:3).
- **Gentleness remembers that we have all sinned and come short of the glory of God** (Romans 3:23), and we are all trying to find our way.
- **Gentleness extends grace** (undeserved favor), love, and kindness to difficult people.
- **Gentleness or a soft answer** turns away anger (Proverbs 15:1).

Gentleness Prayer for My Sister

Father in the name of Jesus, I love You. My sister loves You because You first loved us. It is Your gentleness towards us that leads to repentance. You are so gentle and kind towards us. Lord, if we have not been gentle towards You, others, or even ourselves, then we ask for forgiveness. We ask that You will make us whole. Lord, when we are dealing with our enemies or difficult people, and we become weak, then send us the strength to be gentle. We love You, Lord, and we want to be pleasing to You and bring Your name the glory that belongs to You. Lord, we also know and understand that we are human, so we fall short. We need You to help us! Help us, to exercise the fruit of the spirit called gentleness. Lord, be a present help to us in the name of Jesus Christ. Amen.

MIRROR MOMENT

A
AFFECT
(EMOTIONS)

B
BEHAVIOR
(ACTIONS)

C
COGNITION
(THOUGHTS)

~Reflections ~

SOAP BIBLE STUDY METHOD

S - Scripture

Read the scripture without trying to determine meaning. Just read what is there.

O - Observance

Notice what stands out for you or what captures your attention. Sometimes, using the 5 W's helps with this – who, what, when, where, why, and how?

A - Application

Ask yourself, "so what?" How does this apply to me and my life and how can I utilize it in my life?" Be honest with yourself.

P - Prayer

Pray without ceasing. Pray before. Pray during. Pray afterwards. Be prayerful throughout this process.

SOAP BIBLE STUDY METHOD

S - Scripture   O - Observance

A - Application   P - Prayer

SCRIPTURES ON THIS FRUIT

SEEDS TO PRODUCE MUCH FRUIT

Compass Points

What action(s) were taken? What action(s) do you need to take?

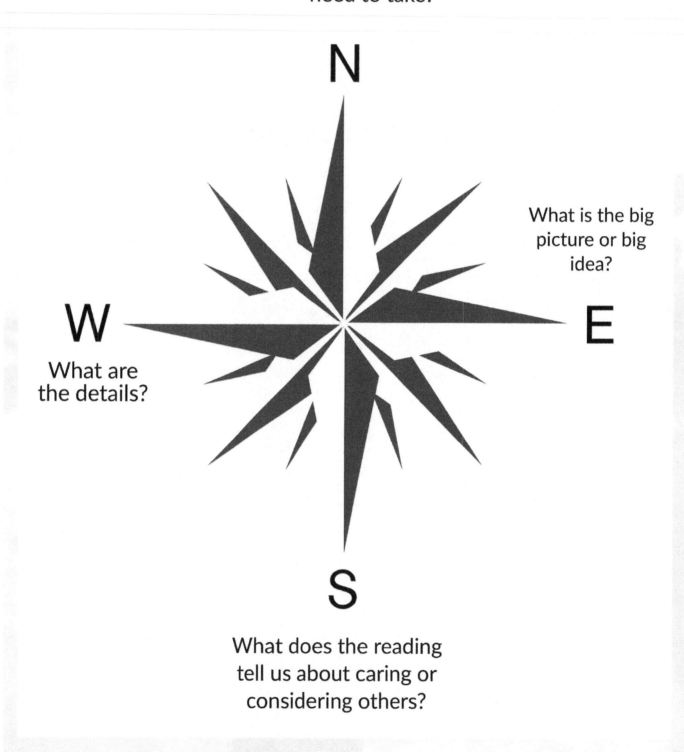

N

What is the big picture or big idea?

E

What are the details?

W

S

What does the reading tell us about caring or considering others?

Note to self

K What do you know?

W What do you want to know?

L What did you learn?

Made in the image of God

Month:

Month:

G

Self-control

HE THAT HATH NO RULE OVER HIS OWN SPIRIT
IS LIKE A CITY THAT IS BROKEN DOWN, AND WITHOUT WALLS. - PROVERBS 25:28

Self-control

HE THAT HATH NO RULE OVER HIS OWN SPIRIT
IS LIKE A CITY THAT IS BROKEN DOWN, AND WITHOUT WALLS. - PROVERBS 25:28

Self-control
By Cassandra Tembo

Growing up we had a saying…"cool, calm, and collected". This was used to describe someone who had things under control and was not prone to emotional outbursts. While this was certainly a desired character trait, I must admit this did not apply to me much of the time. Well into adulthood, I would describe myself as easily excitable on both the positive and negative end of the spectrum. I experienced extreme highs and extreme lows. I vacillated from ecstatic joy to heaviness and even oppression. I would transition from playful jesting to intense seriousness without advanced notice. At times, I managed to conceal it from most people depending on the environment and my disposition at the time. Other times these swings were evident to anyone in my presence. Not exactly the descriptor you would expect for a woman of God in ministry. Certainly not the kind of person you might seek as a close friend.

When I consider the fruit of the Spirit in Galatians 5:22-23, I am reminded that fruit is singular and not plural. All nine attributes listed are one complete package. Despite my inclination to celebrate what I considered strengths while avoiding development in other areas, self-control was always the one that caused me to cringe as I reviewed the list. What is it and why was it so difficult for me to achieve? Proverbs 25:28 offers a good reference for self-control. "He that hath no rule over his own spirit is like a city that is broken down, and without walls." That's exactly how I felt. ***I felt broken...exposed...out of control.***

Self-control is the ability to temper one's heart, mind, and emotions in accordance with God's Word. When we understand and embrace God's instructions and promises, our response to stimuli around us begins to reflect God's heart. Grace, mercy, and love become the guiding principles that rule our spirit. Destructive attitudes and communication give way to healing, restoration, and edification. Our composure in the midst of challenging circumstances builds and fortifies the city instead of breaking down its walls. Tzenuit, the Hebrew word for modesty is commonly translated as self-control. Engkratea is the Greek word which means "inner strength". The Hebrew and Greek terms combine to define self-control as the inner strength needed to control one's passions. It is significant to note self-control is the final attribute listed and in some respects may be the supporting component for the other eight traits.

Understanding the meaning was not difficult but consistently exhibiting self-control was a challenge. I watched others who appeared to manage stressful situations with ease. What was I missing? I believe the key was Zechariah 4:6b, "...Not by might, nor by power, but by My Spirit, saith the Lord of hosts." I like to paraphrase this verse as "Not by *my* might, nor by *my* power, but by *His* Spirit". I discovered self-control is not based on my ability to control anything. It is only achieved by recognizing our inability to control ourselves within our own strength. We must make the conscious decision to release control. We must surrender to Him. Then and only then can we do all things through Christ who strengthens us (Philippians

4:13). Then we will be gentle enough to give a soft answer that turns away wrath (Proverbs 15:1). We will have the stamina to be steadfast, unmoveable, always abounding in the work of the Lord (I Corinthians 15:58). We will be wise as a serpent and harmless as a dove (Matthew 10:16) in the face of opposition. When we allow God to work through us, we will not fall prey to being so self-controlled that we fail to express righteous indignation like Jesus did when He overturned the money tables in the temple to convey His displeasure with inappropriate practices (Matthew 21:12). We will exhibit appropriate balance of emotions, words, and actions in every situation. Moreover, we will please our Heavenly Father as we reflect His love on the earth.

So what was my turning point regarding self-control? When I entered into God's rest as described in Hebrews 4, stress and anxiety dissipated.   I cast my cares upon Him and truly understood just how much He cares for you and me (I Peter 5:7), I no longer felt the pressure to create perfect outcomes. The pressure to be perfect was the catalyst that fueled my counterproductive responses and emotional gyrations. The self-imposed pressure was largely my attempt to live up to what I perceived others expected. All the while, I was not living the abundant life Christ came to give me. I finally understood, self-control was not about me controlling myself.   It was about me giving God control and following His lead to a life of peace and fruitfulness. Do I get it right every time, every day? Certainly not. But I can now read the fruit of the Spirit without cringing at "self-control". We are all on our way to that destination called "there". There's a place God is trying to take us as we yield to His purpose and plan for our life. The fruit of the Spirit will ensure safety for us and those we encounter along the way.

Self-Control Prayer for My Sister

Thank You Lord for helping my sister enter into Your rest and relieve all pressure to control outcomes in ways she was never intended to do. May she find real peace in releasing control to You. Thank You her emotions are perfectly balanced. She responds to situations effortlessly because she is assured You are more than capable and willing to handle everything that concerns her. Therefore, she does not need to experience anxiety or ineffective reactions to life's challenges. Thank You that my sister enjoys a life of temperance as she surrenders control to You, her Lord and Savior. Amen.

MIRROR MOMENT

A
AFFECT
(EMOTIONS)

B
BEHAVIOR
(ACTIONS)

C
COGNITION
(THOUGHTS)

~Reflections ~

SOAP BIBLE STUDY METHOD

S - Scripture

Read the scripture without trying to determine meaning. Just read what is there.

O - Observance

Notice what stands out for you or what captures your attention. Sometimes, using the 5 W's helps with this – who, what, when, where, why, and how?

A - Application

Ask yourself, "so what?" How does this apply to me and my life and how can I utilize it in my life?" Be honest with yourself.

P - Prayer

Pray without ceasing. Pray before. Pray during. Pray afterwards. Be prayerful throughout this process.

SOAP BIBLE STUDY METHOD

S - Scripture   O - Observance

A - Application   P - Prayer

SCRIPTURES ON THIS FRUIT

SEEDS TO PRODUCE MUCH FRUIT

Compass Points

What action(s) were taken? What action(s) do you need to take?

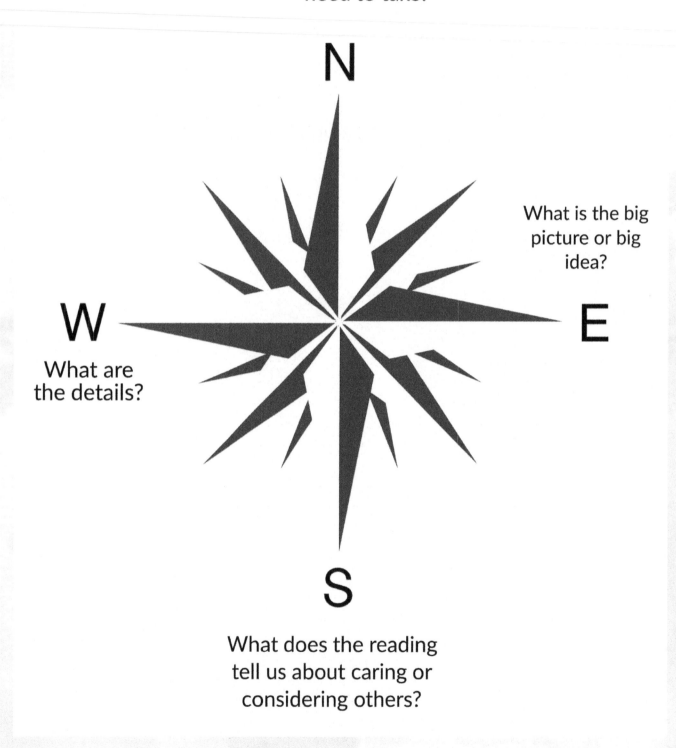

N

What is the big picture or big idea?

E

W

What are the details?

S

What does the reading tell us about caring or considering others?

Note to self

K
What do you know?

W
What do you want to know?

L
What did you learn?

Made in the image of God

Month:

Month:

Notes

Notes

Notes

Notes